Navigating the Interior Life

STUDY GUIDE

Navigating the Interior Life

Spiritual Direction
and the Journey to God

STUDY GUIDE

DANIEL BURKE

TABLE OF CONTENTS

HOW TO USE THIS GUIDE
Suggestions for Individual and Group Study

While many of the exercises in this study guide require solitude and quiet reflection, the material will also lend itself to small group study. It can be very beneficial to discuss many of the concepts introduced in this guide with other like-minded individuals who are on the same path to a deeper union with God.

Regardless of whether you are using this study guide alone or with a group, we highly recommend you read *Navigating the Interior Life* and have it handy so you can refer back to it if you need to. We also recommend using a notebook or journal to record your thoughts.

PRACTICAL TIPS FOR SMALL GROUP STUDY

1. Start and end on time. If you make it a practice right from the start to begin and end on time, you'll show respect for those who show up on time and those who need to leave promptly when the study ends. Sixty to ninety minutes is a good time frame to aim for.

2. Limit the size of the group. Six to eight is a good number; if you have more than this, it will be difficult for everyone to fit around a table or in someone's living room. Too large of a group will make it hard to keep to your schedule and still give everyone time to share during the discussion time.

3. Structure your group to correspond to the chapters in the book. Nine weeks is ideal, or you can choose to combine some of the chapters for a six-to-eight week study.

4. As the facilitator, be sensitive to the personalities of the participants. Make sure each person who wants to share has the opportunity to do so. At times, more talkative members might need a reminder not to monopolize the discussion and more reserved participants might need some encouragement to open up.

5. Respect the confidentiality of the group. You'll be sharing honestly about the deeper issues of your faith, and it's important to establish trust so each participant feels safe opening up. At the same time, not everyone will want to divulge his or her innermost thoughts, and this should be respected too. Keep what is shared in confidence, and make a commitment to pray for each other during the week.

6. If you decide to serve refreshments, participants can take turns bringing something simple to be served at the end. This study requires everyone's full participation and focus, so you'll want to keep distractions to a minimum.

WHAT IS SPIRITUAL DIRECTION?

In its essence, spiritual direction is a relationship with a kind of spiritual coach through which we come to better know, love, and serve Christ. Through the grace and guidance of the Holy Spirit, the director and the directee work together to understand God's will, and then determine how to follow His leading in a concrete way on a day-to-day basis, ultimately seeking to experience the heights of spiritual union with God.

Thomas Dubay shares an experience from his own life to illustrate this relationship:

> Years ago two blind men crossed paths in a drizzle on a neighborhood street in Falkirk, Scotland. The first enjoyed sensory vision and knew in a general way where his destination was, but he did not know how to negotiate the ever-winding streets which abound in old Scottish towns. His blindness was a lack of practical know-how: he was lost. The other man lacked sensory vision, but he was not lost. The first of these two individuals was I. As I drew near to the second, I discovered that he was literally blind, but nonetheless I presented my problem to him. With an extraordinary warmth I shall never forget, he took me by the arm and walked me to the brow of a hill. There he described to me how to find the monastery at which I was to give a series of lectures.[1]

---

1. Thomas Dubay, SM, *Seeking Spiritual Direction: How to Grow the Divine Life Within* (Cincinnati, OH: Servant Books, 1993), 11.

This reflection from a spiritual master of our time illustrates the importance of a spiritual director in helping us to find our destination. In this first chapter, we discuss important concepts regarding what constitutes spiritual direction and the often confused notions that can hinder the seeker from understanding how to best appropriate this gift of the Church.

WHAT SPIRITUAL DIRECTION IS NOT

Before we delve more deeply into what spiritual direction is, it will be helpful to understand what it is *not*. Here are ten key distinctions:

1. **Spiritual direction is not a boss/employee relationship.** In our culture today, we might tend to assume a "director" is someone who tells the one being directed what to do. This is not the case in healthy spiritual direction. Instead, the director/directee relationship is more like that of a personal coach and an athlete.

2. **Spiritual direction is not confession.** In ancient times it was very common for confession and spiritual direction to take place together. But even so, spiritual direction has never been the exclusive territory of priests or religious. A surprising example is St. John Paul II, who, while in his youth, had a lay spiritual director. Today, confession and spiritual direction are usually two separate activities.

3. **Spiritual direction is not friendship.** Spiritual direction differs from spiritual friendship in two key ways. First, the specific focus of spiritual direction is the spiritual life of the directee, period. Second, using the coach/athlete analogy, personal coaching is not about friendship. One engages a personal coach to be challenged, motivated, and encouraged toward concrete progress for which they expect to be held accountable.

4. **Spiritual direction is not a Catholic self-help program.** Our culture places a high value on self-sufficiency, self-reliance, and even self-centeredness, but we should not approach spiritual direction with the idea of receiving a pep talk to enable us to get going on our own again. As St. Bernard said, "He who constitutes himself his own director becomes the disciple of a fool."[2] Spiritual direction is meant to break us of our false reliance on self.

2. Quoted in Adolphe Tanquerey, *The Spiritual Life* (Rockford, IL: Tan Books, reprinted 2000 [original 1930]), no. 533.

5. **Spiritual direction is not psychological counseling.** One's psychological and physical health does have an impact on the spiritual life, but spiritual direction is not designed to address deep psychological issues.

6. **Spiritual direction is not a one-time event.** Spiritual direction is not like a visit to a spiritual emergency room in the midst of a crisis. Rather, it is an ongoing relationship between a wise director and an individual who is ready and willing to work diligently and consistently on their relationship with God.

7. **Spiritual direction is not wandering around with a spiritual companion.** Some modern conceptions of spiritual direction reduce it to mere spiritual meandering and self-discovery. But spiritual direction is meant to be a deliberate journey on a specific path.

8. **Spiritual direction is not just "me and Jesus."** God has chosen to use human instruments to shape, mold, and bring us closer to Him. Discounting the need for human assistance can become a comfortable but dangerous trap.

9. **Spiritual direction is not apostolic work.** If the director and directee are both involved in a particular apostolate, there might be a tendency to focus on the work of that apostolate rather than emphasizing one's relationship with Christ.

10. **Spiritual direction is not just about prayer . . . and not just about action.** If prayer or action are emphasized to the exclusion of the other, it cannot be considered mature spiritual direction. A balanced approach is necessary.

Spiritual direction is a relationship between three persons:

- the Holy Spirit
- the director
- the directee

The main focus of spiritual direction is union with God. The central aim of spiritual direction is to help guide the directee to purposefully, consistently, and substantively grow in their relationship with God and neighbor.

QUESTIONS FOR REFLECTION

Why are you drawn to the idea of spiritual direction?

Did you share any of these common misconceptions about spiritual direction before you reviewed this section? If so, which ones and how did this misconception hinder either your seeking or your effective working experience with spiritual direction?

How have these clarifications helped you to understand what spiritual direction is and how it might benefit you?

If you have experienced spiritual direction, describe the benefits and also any problems you may have encountered.

Describe in your own words what should ideally happen during spiritual direction.

Using your more enhanced view of what spiritual direction is and is not, how might you more effectively approach a spiritual direction relationship based on this perspective?

Is Spiritual Direction Right for You?

Before you can discern if spiritual direction is right for you, another question must be answered: how important is spiritual direction? Isn't it enough to be present at Mass each week, one parishioner among many? If you aspire to more than sitting in a pew week after week, if you are seeking greater awareness of God's presence and activity in your life, then spiritual direction is worth exploring—along with other tools for deepening your spiritual life: prayer, the sacraments (especially the Eucharist and Confession), spiritual reading, and meditation.

DO YOU REALLY NEED SPIRITUAL DIRECTION?

In times past, spiritual direction was not as optional as we think of it today. The saints can shed some light on this for us.

> Do not be your own master and do not set out upon a way that is entirely new for you without a guide; otherwise you will soon go astray. (St. Jerome)

> You wouldn't think of building a good house to live in here on earth without an architect. How can you ever hope, without a director, to build the castle of your sanctification in order to live forever in heaven? (St. Josemaría Escrivá)[1]

> God so desires that man place himself under the direction of another, that He absolutely does not want to see us give full assent

1. St. Jose María Escrivá, *The Way, Furrow, The Forge* (New York: Scepter Books, 2001), 14.

7

to the supernatural truths He Himself imparts, before they have issued out of the mouth of a man. (St. John of the Cross)[2]

To be able to discover the actual will of the Lord in our lives always involves the following: a receptive listening to the Word of God and the Church, fervent and constant prayer, recourse to a wise and loving spiritual guide, and a faithful discernment of the gifts and talents given by God. (St. John Paul II)[3]

The spiritual life is a journey, uncharted territory full of twists and turns. To really make progress and avoid unnecessary pitfalls, it is invaluable to enlist the assistance of an experienced guide. There is simply no way we can know our own blind spots accurately or know where we're headed spiritually without trusted advisors.

ARE YOU READY FOR SPIRITUAL DIRECTION?

Once you've decided that spiritual direction is valuable and important, how do you know if you're ready for it? If you don't explore this question first, you might wander into a relationship with a spiritual director that leaves you more confused and frustrated than before. Fortunately there are signposts along the way that can point you in the right direction.

- *Signpost #1:* You are a committed Catholic, yet you feel a sense of emptiness and stagnation in your faith. You don't seem to be growing or making progress in your spiritual life. You struggle with patterns of sin, often causing you to become discouraged. Your life is not filled with the peace you know Christ promised.
- *Signpost #2:* You are longing for something more. You want to go deeper in prayer, but you're not sure how. You want to engage more fully with Christ. You desire a clearer sense of God's path for your life.
- *Signpost #3:* You have a vibrant, vital faith, but you recognize that you are at a point where you feel that further progress requires

---

2. Quoted in Charles Hugo Doyle, *Guidance in Spiritual Direction* (New York: Roman Catholic Books, 1956), 8.

3. Pope St. John Paul II, Apostolic Exhortation on the Laity *Christifidelis laici* (December 30, 1988), 58.

supernatural energy beyond what you currently have. You sense that the enemy of your soul is aware of you and that you are entering territory that calls for the "whole armor of God."

WHAT IF YOU'RE NOT READY FOR SPIRITUAL DIRECTION?

Even though you are convinced of the value of spiritual direction, you might tell yourself that you're "not ready" for such a commitment. Upon deeper reflection, however, you might discover certain hindrances that cause you to feel this way and prevent you from pursuing this path.

Fr. Reginald Garrigou-Lagrange identified the main source as pride: "Pride is a bandage over the eyes of our spirit, which hinders us from seeking the truth, especially that relative to the majesty of God and the excellence of those who surpass us. It prevents us from wishing to be instructed by them, or it prompts us not to accept direction without argument."[4] Here are four examples:

1. A woman named Kathy attends Mass every day and prays a daily Rosary, and she is proud of being such a committed Catholic. Over time she has overcome a few of her past sin patterns and has come to feel she doesn't need anything else for her spiritual growth. Kathy has fallen prey to a subtle form of pride that leads her to conclude she has no need of a spiritual director.

2. Tom is on an endless search for a spiritual director, never finding one that he considers to be advanced enough to lead him. He thinks only a priest will do, and this form of pride keeps him from forming a relationship with a holy layperson who understands the path of humility and what it means to have a vibrant friendship with Christ. In the meantime, he is stalled in his spiritual growth.

3. Karen sees the value of spiritual direction, but she holds herself back because she is not willing to enter into the openness and transparency needed for true spiritual progress. Instead, she wants to look good in the eyes of others (vanity)—in effect choosing appearances over baring her soul truthfully. When she has entered into spiritual direction, her director was not able to help her make much progress.

---

4. Reginald Garrigou-Lagrange, *The Three Ages of the Interior Life* (Rockford, IL: Tan Books, 1989), 381.

4. Don's problem is spiritual sloth. He knows he should find a spiritual director, but he never gets around to it. The cares and distractions of his busy life lull him into spiritual laziness and mediocrity. Leo, on the other hand, entered into spiritual direction thinking that the director will now take control of his spiritual life while he goes along for the ride.

No matter what the areas of weakness you encounter, the truth remains: we are all called to a deeper relationship with Christ. Make the commitment to forge ahead, reaping the benefits of being open and honest with your spiritual director.

QUESTIONS FOR REFLECTION

How might spiritual direction assist you to better recognize your blind spots?

Since blind spots are outside our vision (we can't see them on our own), how have you become aware of yours?

Describe how you perceive the value of an objective viewpoint (who understands and is advanced in the spiritual life) regarding the state of your soul and what you may need to change to make progress.

Which of the three signposts listed above best describes you?

If you feel you might not be ready for spiritual direction, do you see yourself in the examples of Kathy, Tom, Karen, Don, or Leo? Which one can you relate to the most?

Take some time to pray about moving forward with spiritual direction. Where would spiritual direction possibly help you most in your spiritual journey?

FINDING A SPIRITUAL DIRECTOR

A spiritual director can be a priest, a religious, or a layperson. The ideal is to have a well-trained spiritual director who is also a confessor, but this isn't always possible. It's more important that the spiritual director you choose has received extensive personal spiritual formation, along with training in the art of spiritual direction—specifically training that is faithful to the magisterium. Not all spiritual directors or schools for spiritual direction embrace authentic Catholic spirituality, so as you begin your search you want to avoid harmful New Age or non-Catholic spirituality disguised as Catholic teaching. The kind of person you want for a spiritual director should be knowledgeable about the faith and the spiritual life, and also practical, balanced, and trustworthy.

PREPARE FOR THE SEARCH

To be up for the challenge of finding a spiritual director, the seeker must focus his or her energies on the ultimate goal of an intimate union with Christ. This involves intellectual formation through spiritual reading and study, which leads to the maturity that is able to discern truth from error. This lifelong habit is one of the keys to successfully navigating around the present dangers of human weakness and deception (including self-deception).

So then, what should you read? In addition to Bible study, *The Catechism of the Catholic Church* is extremely valuable, especially Part IV on the subject of prayer. Church documents and papal encyclicals are rich treasures of wisdom. Additionally, the Doctors of the Church (St. Teresa of Avila, St. John of the Cross, St. Francis de Sales, St. Bernard of Clairvaux, St. Catherine of Siena, St. Thérèse of Lisieux, St. John of Avila and St. Hildegard of Bingen) have all written extensively on the topics of prayer and the spiritual life. To round out your spiritual reading, many contemporary authors are trustworthy sources for authentic Catholic spirituality. These include Dr. Ralph Martin, Fr. Thomas Dubay, Fr. Jacques Philippe, Fr. John Bartunek, and Fr. Benedict Groeschel.

Spiritual reading is a powerful weapon in the spiritual warfare that is sure to come when you are truly serious about your spiritual life. It provides a sure foundation from which to begin your search for a spiritual director who is right for you.

FINDING THE REAL THING

Let's be clear: finding the right spiritual director is *not* easy, but always remember, God knows what you need even before you ask Him. "Before they call, I will answer," He says (Isaiah 65:24). Even your heartfelt desire to deepen your spiritual life comes from God, and He will guide you to a spiritual director who can satisfy that desire.

Contacting your local diocesan office or your parish priest are good places to begin. You can also ask those you know who have a deep spirituality and are growing. There's a good chance they may have a spiritual director, or know someone who can recommend one.

Don't rush the process; it can be a long one. The Holy Spirit will guide you, and sometimes the search itself can be just as valuable as spiritual direction itself.

Some questions to ask prospective spiritual directors to determine if they are a good fit for you:

- Are you in spiritual direction yourself? How often do you meet with your director?
- Are there any teachings of the Catholic Church that you disagree with or struggle with?
- What theological or spiritual formation and/or special training do you have that qualifies you as a spiritual director?
- How would you describe your relationship with Christ?

You might feel uncomfortable asking these questions, but it's much better to do your homework on the front end as opposed to having to disengage from a relationship with a director down the road when you realize you made the wrong choice.

A busy mom with six young children shares her own experience of finding a spiritual director:

> From my own experience, finding a spiritual director was a bit of work. It's definitely awkward (for people like me, anyway) to start calling around and setting up meetings with people you don't even know. That was a big mental block I had to overcome. Then I was bound and determined that I wanted a priest or a religious brother or sister as a spiritual director. When my priest gave me the phone number of a local laywoman who is trained in spiritual direction and strongly urged me to consider her, I didn't plan to call—I was that sure that I didn't want a layperson. But then something nagged at me about it, and I decided to just set up one meeting to see how it went. As it turns out, she could not have been a better fit for me, and I am thrilled to have her as my spiritual director.
>
> So to summarize the lessons I learned from my own experience: just pray, pray, pray for God to lead you to the right person; be open to the promptings of the Holy Spirit, even if he leads you in a direction you didn't expect; and be willing to put in a little effort—it will pay off in a big way when you finally find the right person![1]

St. Symeon the New Theologian offers some wise advice for choosing a spiritual director:

> Seek out one who is, if you will, an intercessor, a physician, and a good counselor; a good counselor, that he may offer ways of repentance which agree with his good advice; a physician, that he may prescribe the appropriate medicine for each of your wounds; and an intercessor, that he may propitiate God, standing before Him face to face, and offering Him prayer and intercession on your behalf.[2]

---

1. Jennifer Fulwiler, http://www.conversiondiary.com/2009/01/how-to-find-a-spiritual-director.html.

2. J. Chryssavgis, *Soul Mending: The Art of Spiritual Direction* (Brookline, MA: Holy Cross Orthodox Press, 2000), 207.

QUESTIONS FOR REFLECTION

How committed are you to finding a spiritual director? On a scale of one to ten, with one being only slightly committed and ten being totally committed, rate yourself. Now list the reasons you feel the way you do.

What are you most hoping to get out of spiritual direction?

Are you intimidated by the idea of "interviewing" a potential spiritual director? Why or why not?

Does it matter to you if your spiritual director is a priest or a layperson? Male or female? Older or younger than you? Describe why you feel the way you do.

Are you willing to travel to meet with your director? How ready are you to suffer whatever discomfort you may encounter for the greater end of finding peace of soul and living life according to your ultimate purpose?

Is it important that your spiritual director also be your confessor? Why or why not?

PREPARING FOR SPIRITUAL DIRECTION

You've found a spiritual director and set an appointment for your first meeting. You're excited . . . and a little apprehensive. This is perfectly normal. The process and nature of spiritual growth is uncharted ground—an unknown. It's a bit like heading into a tunnel; we are compelled to keep moving, but what we might encounter as we make our way through it is uncertain, even uncomfortable. But keep the end in mind—greater intimacy with God and union with His will—and be encouraged that God is calling you forward and you are listening to Him.

YOUR FIRST MEETING

Once you've identified a prospective spiritual director, set up a short, thirty-minute meeting to briefly discuss your spiritual life. Prepare for the meeting by planning to limit the discussion to very specific goals or challenges you are facing spiritually. For instance, you might say, "I am struggling with my prayer life." This should be all that a wise spiritual director needs to help you identify and overcome the challenges you face. It's beneficial to write down any items you wish to discuss; this will help you to clarify the specific issues you want to cover.

Note: Always arrive before your scheduled time—never make your spiritual director wait for you. In addition, clarify the end time with the director; this is another way of respecting his or her time.

When your session is finished, make a point of writing down and repeating back to your director the direction you received. Show that you have been actively listening by asking the director: "Have I understood you correctly?"

While it's always optimal to meet face-to-face, at times you might schedule some follow-up or in-between sessions by phone or email or Skype, especially if the traveling distance between you and your director is significant.

Consider making a donation at the conclusion of your session, even if the spiritual director does not charge for direction. If the director is a priest or a religious, sometimes a donation to their order will be appropriate.

If your initial session has gone well and you want to continue the relationship, try to schedule a time for your next meeting right then and there, choosing a specific date and time. This is similar to scheduling a follow-up appointment with your doctor or dentist; you don't leave it to chance or it might never happen.

THE SPIRITUAL DIRECTOR'S RESPONSIBILITIES

Remember that managing your spiritual growth is *not* your spiritual director's responsibility. However, spiritual directors do have their own set of responsibilities. These include maturing in their own faith; receiving spiritual direction themselves; growing in the virtues; increasing in the knowledge of Church teaching; and deepening their prayer life.

During the spiritual direction session, good spiritual directors will:

- Have the awareness that they are instruments of the Holy Spirit, not the leading actor in the relationship;
- Prayerfully listen to the promptings of the Holy Spirit to uncover the root issues that hinder your progress;
- Listen to discern what you really mean, not just what you say;
- Gently but firmly challenge you to be open, honest, accountable, and faithful to what God is asking of you;
- Ensure that the spiritual direction relationship never crosses appropriate personal boundaries.

Spiritual directors are imperfect humans, and you might discover that yours is stronger in certain areas than others. But if you understand how spiritual direction can and should work, you can do your part to make sure the process is a fruitful one.

YOUR RESPONSIBILITIES IN SPIRITUAL DIRECTION

It's up to you to take complete ownership of your spiritual growth. Remember, your spiritual director is not like a physician who keeps a chart of your progress. It is better to keep your own chart, journal, and notes. You are responsible for reviewing your notes prior to each session and updating them at the end of the meeting. And just like with the doctor-patient relationship, you make your appointments and keep them.

Beyond these basics, there are some key aspects that you are also responsible for.

You should be *docile and obedient.* This can easily be misunderstood today in our society that values autonomy and independence. While you should always maintain your freedom to act according to your own will and the teachings of the Church, you should also maintain an equal readiness to humbly accept the insight and direction of a director who is worthy of your trust. Docility is the humble readiness to follow God's will for your life. This might be expressed by your willingness to listen to and follow imperfect counsel from an imperfect person, even when you disagree or don't fully understand. It can be a profound act of holiness to obey your spiritual director, particularly when he or she suggests something difficult, which can often lead you into a deeper relationship with Christ. God never usurps our free will, and neither should a spiritual director. If the spiritual direction relationship is healthy, your spiritual director won't exert influence over your life without your consent.

Jesus Himself provided us with this model: "He went down with them and came to Nazareth, and was obedient to them. . . . And Jesus increased in wisdom and stature, and in favor with God and man" (Luke 2:51–52).

Openness is also a vital aspect of a spiritual directee. As St. John Climacus wrote: "A pilot cannot save a ship on his own without the assistance of his sailors. Nor can a physician cure a patient unless he is entreated . . . by the sick person who in complete confidence reveals the wound."[1]

A common tragedy in the spiritual life occurs when we know we need help, but we prefer to suffer in our misery rather than entrust ourselves to someone

---

1. Ibid., 180.

who might be able to come to our aid. Instead, we hide our pain under a cloak of denial while a spiritual cancer eats away at our souls.

Tina is an example of this. A model in her parish community, she was a master of good works and was always busy serving the Church in some capacity. No one knew that deep inside a hidden, habitual sin was weakening her, chipping away at the bridge of grace to God. Eventually she found that bridge had become weak and impassable, and she had a crisis of faith. Fortunately, Tina knew where to turn; she went to Confession and she found a spiritual director she trusted enough to be open and transparent with, and she was able to experience healing and growth.

PREPARATION IS KEY

It is disrespectful to your director and a waste of time to come unprepared to your spiritual direction appointment. Preparation really starts as you leave your last appointment, when you jot down the insights you received. These might include:

- "Discouragement never comes from God."
- "I'm impatient because I'm arrogant."
- "I neglect spiritual practices because I only do what I feel like doing."

Preparation also includes deciding on some concrete actions you plan to work on over the next month. For instance:

- "I will spend the first five minutes of my day thanking God for today's blessings."
- "I will respond patiently when I'm stuck in traffic instead of lashing out."
- "I will set a schedule for morning prayer and stick to it."

The day before your spiritual direction appointment, look at your notes and assess your progress, asking the Holy Spirit for light. You might say:

- "I really made progress here. Why? What made the difference?"
- "When such-and-such happened, it totally derailed me. Why?"
- "I made no progress on this point. Why?"

Asking "why" is an important part of your analysis. It will give you questions to discuss with your director, basically setting the agenda for your upcoming session.

As you prepare for spiritual direction, you'll want to think about the following things since your last spiritual direction session:

- The general state of your soul since your last meeting
- Difficulties or failures in your moral life
- Progress made or not made since your last session
- Result of concrete actions you took
- Challenges in your prayer life
- The quality of the key relationships and responsibilities of your state in life

Just as infrequent exercise doesn't do much good and frequent exercise provides lasting benefits, so too infrequent spiritual direction sessions yield inconsistent progress and regular meetings provide continual gains. Once you're committed to a spiritual direction relationship, make sure you set up regular meetings with your director, even if this poses some difficulty. A good rule of thumb is to meet every three to four weeks in the beginning, and once the relationship is established, every four to six weeks or even once a quarter is sufficient if all is going well.

QUESTIONS FOR REFLECTION

If you've been in a spiritual direction relationship, how did you keep track of the insights you received and the progress you planned to make?

What specific life issues are you currently facing that would benefit from a conversation with your spiritual director?

How would you describe your relationship with God at the moment?

How open or responsive have you been to the leading of the Holy Spirit in your life, and what has been the result?

What is the state of your prayer life currently?

What events, experiences, or relationships have communicated to you a sense of God's presence? His absence?

SPIRITUAL SELF-EVALUATION

Spiritual direction can be compared to a good rearview mirror and a clean windshield. The rearview mirror provides a healthy perspective of our past, while the windshield gives us a clear view of what lies ahead. Certain exercises and tools are beneficial to make sure you have the best possible visibility on your spiritual journey. During a retreat, for instance, you can gain a heightened awareness of your spiritual state. In an environment where you can escape the distractions and noise of normal daily life, you can enter a state of quiet reflection, begin to really hear God's voice, and be able to evaluate your life in a deeply meaningful way.

If you are unable to attend a retreat, you can create your own "retreat" by setting aside several hours on a weekend. You can visit a church where you can sit silently before the Blessed Sacrament. Invite the Holy Spirit to help you evaluate your life. The following exercises are designed to help you do this.

YOUR SPIRITUAL HERITAGE

In order to increase your awareness of God's presence in your life, it's helpful to write a brief description of your spiritual journey. You can divide your life into major periods (birth to age twelve; your teen years; your twenties and thirties; and so on) and then highlight the key moments that were significant spiritually. (Remember, you're not writing an extensive autobiography here—you are identifying the highlights that shaped your spiritual awareness.) Here are some questions to get you started.

How would you describe your parents' influence?

Describe their spiritual journey if you can. How did they live?

What did they teach you about God and faith?

Who other than your parents influenced you the most spiritually? What did they teach you?

When did you first learn about God? How did you perceive Him?

What was your life like in terms of virtue, strengths, weaknesses, and interests?

Were there any particular challenges or trials you experienced? What affect did they have on you?

YOUR SPIRITUAL STATUS

Once you've completed the above exercise, take some time to honestly evaluate where you are now spiritually. Be aware of any temptation to be overly self-critical; there will always be areas for improvement, and patience with yourself is necessary. Take a look at the foundational areas of your faith life: your relationship with Christ, your sacramental participation, your prayer life, and your spiritual and intellectual development. The goal is to simply identify where you are *now* so you can effectively move forward in your spiritual quest. The following questions and charts may prove helpful.

Your Relationship with Christ

How would you describe your relationship with Christ? Is it "personal," or does Jesus seem distant?

Describe your sense of Christ's presence to you—is it constant, or only in rare situations, or somewhere in between?

Is your faith an expression of love and devotion to Christ, or do you perceive it as a duty?

Do you obey God's commands out of fear, or are you compelled out of a sense of love and gratitude?

Your Sacramental Participation

Describe the importance in your life of attending Mass? Do you see it as an obligation or a privilege?

Do you make excuses not to attend Mass on Sunday? If so, outside of illness or work obligations, describe those things that you find more important than the Holy Mass and receiving the Lord of the Universe in the Eucharist.

When you are at Mass, do you fully enter into the liturgy, participating in the responses and singing? Do you daydream, or do you prayerfully engage in each segment?

Do you view Confession as an important practice? Why or why not?

Do you experience resistance to going to Confession? If so, describe how you feel.

How frequently do you participate in the sacraments—in particular Confession and Communion—and Eucharistic Adoration? Use the following chart to help you.

	Daily	Weekly	Monthly	Quarterly	Annually	Other/Don't Know
Eucharist/ Mass						
Adoration						
Reconciliation/ Confession						

Your Prayer Life

What forms of prayer do you enjoy most, and why?

What kinds of prayer do you struggle with most? Describe how. Why do you feel that way?

Do you look forward to prayer, or do you struggle with prayer in general? If yes, in what ways?

Has your prayer deepened or progressed over the years, or is it stagnant? Use the following chart to help you.

	Daily	Weekly	Monthly	Quarterly	Annually	Other/ Don't Know
I pray vocal prayer (Rosary, other formula prayers)						
I practice mental prayer						
I practice an examination of conscience						
Other						

Your Spiritual/Intellectual Development

Do you read and study your Bible? If your answer is no, why not?

What kinds of spiritual books do you read and how frequently?

Are you familiar with the Catechism of the Catholic Church? Do you see it as relevant to your life, or meant only for theologians? Why or why not?

Do you attend any Bible studies or small groups offered in your parish? Why or why not?

If you do attend Bible studies or small groups, what benefits do you receive? How has this impacted your faith formation?

How would you describe the state of your faith formation intellectually? (You can use the following chart as a guide.)

I read...	Daily	Weekly	Monthly	Quarterly	Annually	Other/ Don't Know
Scripture						
Spiritual books						
Theological, apologetics, other Catholic materials						

IDENTIFYING YOUR ROOT SIN

What is a "root sin"? If you are new to the process of spiritual direction, this might be a new concept for you. Classic writings on the spiritual life might refer to this as a "ruling passion," "predominant fault," or "dominant defect." No matter what it's called, the familiar phrase "getting to the root of the problem" expresses the basic idea.

For example, Jane, a young mother with three small children, often finds herself feeling irritable, impatient, and unhappy. She loves God and she wants to be a good mother, but no matter how much she focuses on trying to be good-natured, patient, and happy, she ends up confessing the same sins over and over in confession, and she is frustrated by her inability to find a lasting solution.

Or, Bob has a good job in the corporate world. Although he likes what he does and makes a good salary, his colleagues often find him difficult to get along with. He has a hard time delegating responsibilities to others, thinking that he can do whatever needs to be done better than anyone else. He also is critical of his co-workers and experiences resistance whenever his boss tells him to do something. As a committed Catholic, Bob struggles with these issues but never seems to make progress in overcoming them.

A problem at the *root* of a tree is manifested in the *fruit* of the tree—usually in the lack of fruit. The condition of the fruit is a symptom of the condition of the roots. To solve this problem, we must first recognize the symptoms and then deal with the roots.

Depending on which spiritual tradition we draw from, there are many ways to classify, categorize, and understand root sins. You can find an overview in the Catechism beginning in paragraph 1846. In this study guide, we'll keep it as simple as possible and consider three basic categories of root sin: *pride*, *vanity*, and *sensuality*.

A LOOK AT PRIDE, VANITY, AND SENSUALITY

As we begin to examine the three root sins as well as their most common manifestations, some warm-up questions might be helpful. Make sure you are in a quiet place (ideally with Christ in adoration). Pray and ask the Holy Spirit to give you wisdom and insight, and then just sit quietly for several minutes before you begin. Keep things simple—don't be too concerned with distinctions between the three root sins. Because of our fallen human nature, pride, vanity, and sensuality are present in all of us, but usually one predominates. That's the goal of this exercise: identifying your *predominant* root sin.

Here's a prayer to help you begin:

> *Lord, help me to see the obstacles in me that get in the way of my growth in love and service to You and others. Help me to see the things that I have chosen that keep me from You. Help me to see the things that I may have not deliberately chosen that keep me from You. Help me to be honest with myself and see clearly where You desire to set me free and then help me to be courageous and ruthless in rooting out the darkness and allowing Your light to heal me and draw me firmly onto the path of life. Amen.*

Now you're ready to answer the following questions. Take time to prayerfully review them and then answer each one with a brief paragraph.

Root Sin Evaluation Warm-up Questions

To what do my thoughts naturally tend? What are the preoccupations of my heart? What keeps me up at night? Where do my thoughts and desires spontaneously take me when I am alone or without distractions?

What is generally the cause or source of my sadness, my anxiety, my frustration, my lack of peace, my joy, or my pleasure?

When I have knowingly sinned or disobeyed God, what was the sin or what was my motivation to sin? What are the patterns of sins that show up regularly in confession? Is there a sin or an issue that I regularly bring up in confession?

If and when I have resisted or avoided God in any way, how have I done so? What was at the bottom of my motivation? Why did I do it? What temporal benefit did I gain from the resistance or avoidance?

Root Sin Manifestations

Once you've answered the warm-up questions, you're ready to begin your review of the root sins and their manifestations. If you have seen any of the manifestations in yourself, simply check them off upon your first pass through. Once you have completed your first pass, stop and pray again. Sit in silence for a time and ask the Holy Spirit to guide you.

Take another look at the warm-up questions and then review the checklists. This time work more slowly through the lists, putting a star next to those symptoms that most frequently appear in your life. You should begin to notice more stars or checkmarks appearing in one of the three root sin categories. This is the place to begin your next battle against sin in your life. Be encouraged! Through this exercise, the Holy Spirit is leading you into a new phase of progress and growth.

Never	Sometimes	Frequently	Focus	**Manifestations of the Root Sin of Pride**
				1st Review: Move quickly and assess by instinct. If you hesitate, go with your first instinct. *2nd Review: Review items checked in Sometimes or Frequently categories. Determine manifestations that require attention and identify them in Focus column with a checkmark.*
				too high an opinion of myself or an elevated concept of myself
				annoyance with those who contradict me or question what I say
				inability to submit to those who I judge as less competent or less spiritual than I am
				refusing or resisting assent to others without a satisfactory explanation
				anger if I don't get my way or am not taken into account
				easily judgmental, putting others down, gossiping about them
				slow to recognize or acknowledge my own mistakes or weaknesses
				slow to see when I hurt others and and inability to seek and give forgiveness
				frustration or anger when others don't thank me for favors or work that I do
				unwillingness to serve, rebellion against what I don't like or agree with
				impatience, distance, brusqueness in my daily contact with others
				thinking I am the only one who knows how to do things right
				unwillingness to let others help me or advise me
				inflated idea of my own intelligence and understanding
				dismissing what I do not understand or what others see differently
				not feeling a need for God, even though I do say prayers
				nursing grudges, even in small matters
				never taking orders or bristling when orders are given to me
				inflexible in preferences or perspective
				always putting myself and my things first
				indifference towards others and their needs, never putting myself out for them

Never	Sometimes	Frequently	Focus	**Manifestations of the Root Sin of Pride**
				1st Review: Move quickly and assess by instinct. If you hesitate, go with your first instinct. *2nd Review: Review items checked in Sometimes or Frequently categories. Determine manifestations that require attention and identify them in Focus column with a checkmark.*
				centering everything (conversation, choices, recreation, etc.) on myself and my likes
				calculating in my relations with God and with others

Never	Sometimes	Frequently	Focus	**Manifestations of the Root Sin of Vanity**
				1st Review: Move quickly and assess by instinct. If you hesitate, go with your first instinct. *2nd Review: Review items checked in Sometimes or Frequently categories. Determine manifestations that require attention and identify them in Focus column with a checkmark.*
				always seeking admiration and praise, worrying about not getting it
				excessive concern about physical appearance
				dedicating excessive time to "primping" one's person or possessions
				hoping "I am the best" and finding ways to get others to think so
				being guided by the opinions of others rather than principle
				some types of shyness out of fear of not being liked/accepted by others
				sacrificing principles in order to fit in
				placing too high a premium on popularity and acceptance
				easily discouraged at my failures
				hypocrisy or two-facedness in order to be accepted
				taking pleasure in listening to gossip
				taking pleasure in hearing about or speaking about others' failures or misfortunes
				breaking confidences
				stretching the truth or outright lying to be admired or to hide shortcomings
				severe disappointment when others don't appreciate my ideas or possessions

Never	Sometimes	Frequently	Focus	**Manifestations of the Root Sin of Vanity** *1st Review: Move quickly and assess by instinct. If you hesitate, go with your first instinct.* *2nd Review: Review items checked in Sometimes or Frequently categories. Determine manifestations that require attention and identify them in Focus column with a checkmark.*
				always wanting to be the center of attention, at times stretching the truth or lying outright, or being uncharitable in my words in order to achieve this

Never	Sometimes	Frequently	Focus	**Manifestations of the Root Sin of Sensuality** *1st Review: Move quickly and assess by instinct. If you hesitate, go with your first instinct.* *2nd Review: Review items checked in Sometimes or Frequently categories. Determine manifestations that require attention and identify them in Focus column with a checkmark.*
				laziness
				always seeking comfort, that which requires the least effort
				not going the extra mile for others
				procrastination, last minute in everything
				shoddiness, complaining, excessively affected by minor discomforts
				inability to sacrifice
				not doing my part at home
				always expecting everyone else to serve me
				behavior and decisions ruled by my feelings and moods instead of my principles
				daydreaming a lot with self at the center
				unable to control my thoughts when they attract me, even when they are not good
				doing or partaking only in what I enjoy (food, drink, work, etc.)
				allowing what I enjoy or prefer to push out what I should do
				uncontrolled curiosity, wanting to see/experience everything
				senses and impulses overrule what I know is right and wrong
				acting out feelings (frustrations, desires, etc.) with no regard for God or others
				only working with those I like, being easily hurt

Never	Sometimes	Frequently	Focus	**Manifestations of the Root Sin of Sensuality**
				1st Review: Move quickly and assess by instinct. If you hesitate, go with your first instinct. *2nd Review: Review items checked in Sometimes or Frequently categories. Determine manifestations that require attention and identify them in Focus column with a checkmark.*
				fickleness and inconsistency
				unable to stay on track without constant supervision
				can never finish what I start

THE PATH OF REAL SPIRITUAL GROWTH

Once you've completed the above exercise, you should have a reasonable idea of what your root sin is. But is this new knowledge enough to experience real spiritual growth? Is it enough to "just say no" to our root sins? Is it enough to feel sorrow and then exercise resolve in resisting our root sin?

In 2 Corinthians 7:9–11, St. Paul describes two kinds of repentance, two kinds of sorrow in reaction to sin. One brings life to the soul; the other leads to despair and spiritual death. As you evaluate your root sin and examine your soul before God, there are two paths you can follow. The first is merely recognizing your sin and feeling remorse for it, without actually turning away from it or choosing a new path. This is an incomplete repentance.

The second path is one of true, complete repentance. Here you recognize your sin before God and feel godly sorrow in light of His unlimited mercy and love. You move from mere recognition to action, likely involving confession and penance.

QUESTIONS FOR REFLECTION

As you worked through the questions and identified your root sin, how did you feel? Did you experience a sense of relief or clarity?

Describe the kind of remorse you feel as you take an honest look at the root sin you struggle most with. Were you inclined to turn to God's mercy and forgiveness—or did you feel some resistance to this? Why?

How might identifying your root sin lead you to deeper growth and authenticity as a person?

BEYOND SIN TO VIRTUE AND HOLINESS

Through the previous exercises to identify your root sin, the groundwork has been laid for a real and substantive turning toward God in true repentance. This chapter will provide a practical approach to develop virtue and holiness. The good news is that the call to holiness is not a command you must execute on your own through a sheer act of your will; instead, this comes with the promise of mercy and supernatural assistance. As St. Paul tells us:

> Put off the old man that belongs to your former manner of life and is corrupt through deceitful lusts, and be renewed in the spirit of your minds, and put on the new man, created after the likeness of God in true righteousness and holiness. (Ephesians 4:22–24)

The New Testament is full of similar exhortations. The basic pattern is this: turn *from* sin and turn *to* virtue. That's what you'll do next. You've identified your root sin; now it's time to identify the opposing virtue.

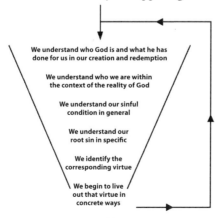

41

A GROWTH IN UNDERSTANDING

As you pursue God and the Church, the sacraments, prayer, Scripture, study, and spiritual reading, you begin to understand God better. You discover how much He loves you and how much He's done for you as an individual, all within the context of your needs and struggles from day to day.

This understanding naturally leads to a shift in your understanding of who you are. Your identity begins to take shape within the context of who God is and how He is working, loving, breathing, and living within you.

Another understanding begins to develop: you become aware of how you are succeeding and struggling in your efforts to deepen your relationship with God. You begin to see and understand what hinders or damages your friendship and intimacy with Him. This often leads to seeking out a spiritual director and understanding your root sin and how it is specifically manifested.

IDENTIFYING THE CORRESPONDING VIRTUE

Ultimately, the goal is to live a positive life of virtue—not a life focused on sin and failure. Once you've identified your root sin, you naturally will concentrate on eliminating it. The process as a whole should be a positive, active, living path, not a negative one.

It is critical, therefore, to focus the vast majority of your energy on the forward pursuit of virtue, not on the sins, sinful inclinations, or attachments of the present or past. Your sin will provide the signposts on your path to help you know which battles you're called to fight on the narrow way leading to God, yet it should never be the primary focus of your energy.

For example, Carole shared with her spiritual director that she has been struggling with a particular manifestation of vanity. She is very successful in her field and is used to receiving awards and public praise for her accomplishments. She enjoys this recognition so much that she constantly seeks ways to draw attention to her achievements. Her director was able to help Carole to identify a corresponding path of virtue: to focus specifically on helping others to succeed, to avoid any effort to take credit, and to give proper accolades to others whenever possible. Carole also decided that she would solve problems and serve others without letting them know what she had done. She planned to quietly make donations and contributions to her favorite charities without letting her friends know.

CREATING A SPECIFIC PLAN

The following is how a specific plan to deal with this type of hindrance to spiritual growth might look.

Root Sin: Vanity

Manifestation: When I accomplish anything good, I am always looking around for praise. Sometimes I fail to acknowledge the contribution of others in my work. At times I have gone so far as to stretch the truth regarding my real accomplishments.

Opposite Virtues: Modesty and Humility

Plan of Action Toward God

- I will meditate on and memorize a passage of Scripture on the humility of Christ as expressed in Philippians 2.

- I will pray the humility prayer every day in the morning for at least the next thirty days.

- I will examine my conscience at the end of each day and write down my failures and successes in following this plan. I will thank and praise Him for my successes and ask forgiveness for my failures.

- I will review my daily notes with my spiritual director at the end of each week.

- I will go to confession if I stray too far off this path.

Plan of Action Toward Others

- I will do at least one work of charity each day and specifically avoid telling anyone under any circumstance. I will not even hint at the good I have done.

- If my good works are noticed, I will say, "Only by His grace" and purposefully change the subject to cast light on something good accomplished by someone else.

Be as specific as possible in your commitment to pursue virtue and avoid sin. Otherwise, it will be very difficult for you to determine if you are successful or not at the end of each day. To the degree you are specific, you will be accountable; to the degree you are accountable, you will be humble and dependent; to the degree you are humble and dependent, you will receive the grace you need to overcome sin and exercise virtue.

Remember, too, that there are no cookie-cutter formulas for this type of soul cleansing. Your soul is unique and different from everyone else's—more so even than your facial qualities. Every battle, though it has similarities to those experienced by others, is unique to you as an individual. Each of us needs to outline a plan that is customized to our own situation under the guidance of the Holy Spirit and a holy spiritual director.

QUESTIONS FOR REFLECTION

If you were to explain your root sin to someone who didn't know you well, how would you do it?

What is your root sin? How does it manifest itself in your daily life? List the ways it affects your relationship with God, with yourself, and with others.

What particular virtue do you desire to live out in a specific way?

How would this particular virtue manifest itself in your daily life?

At the end of the day, how will you know that you've actually lived out this virtue? What questions might you ask yourself to determine if you've lived your commitment toward God? Toward yourself? Toward others?

THE THREE WAYS OF THE
SPIRITUAL LIFE: FINDING YOUR PLACE

Many saints have sought to define and describe the progressive, multi-stage development of the spiritual life. St. Thomas Aquinas provides a profound yet simple summary of the three stages of the spiritual life:

> The first duty which is incumbent on man is to give up sin and resist concupiscence, which are opposed to charity; this belongs to beginners, in whose hearts charity is to be nursed and cherished lest it be corrupted. The second duty of man is to apply his energies chiefly to advance in virtue; this belongs to those who are making progress and who are principally concerned that charity may be increased and strengthened in them. The third endeavor and pursuit of man should be to rest in God and enjoy Him; and this belongs to the perfect who desire to be dissolved and to be with Christ.[1]

The saints predominantly used some form of these three phases: *purgative, illuminative*, and *unitive*—words that describe what happens at each stage. Because these are unfamiliar words to our contemporary ears, we often employ another set of terms that signify a person's spiritual maturity at each stage: *childhood, adolescence*, and *adulthood*. In this study guide, we'll use these terms interchangeably.

---

1. Charles George Herbermann, *The Catholic Encyclopedia, An International Work of Reference on the Constitution, Doctrine,discipline, and History of the Catholic Church* (NY: The Encyclopedia Press, 1914), Vol 14, 254.

> Phase 1: Purgative Way (Childhood)
>
> Phase 2: Illuminative Way (Adolescence)
>
> Phase 3: Unitive Way (Adulthood)

You might be wondering how to determine what stage you are in. Is there some action, a particular disposition, or something else that lets you know you've entered into the ways—or the "interior life of God"? The answer is an emphatic "yes." St. Teresa of Avila described the soul as a castle, with each room reflecting a different level of prayer and virtue on the path toward union with God. She said the two basic elements to gain entry to the castle are "prayer and reflection."

> *Prayer.* The Catechism (2559) says that the essence of prayer is "the raising of one's mind and heart to God." A clear entry into the castle is not reflected by superficial, fleeting prayers gasped just as we narrowly miss an accident on the highway. This is a door we *enter*, not one we merely glance at or peek into. Entering this door is an act of commitment to delve into an active relationship with Christ, one that reflects substantial, consistent effort and persistence through inevitable trials and setbacks.

> *Reflection.* This reflection is the practice of thoughtfully and purposefully seeking to understand ourselves with respect to both the glory of God within us and the results of the fall and sin on our present path to God. The end of healthy reflection is always increased self-awareness, increased humility, and deepened gratitude for the great work of salvation that God continues to work in us. If our reflection results in anything less, then we are merely exercising a shallow, narcissistic overview rather than an in-depth, God-ward evaluation. A God-ward evaluation will always lead us deeper into union with God.

If you've never had the opportunity to study mystical or ascetical theology, a number of the terms and ideas summarized might be unfamiliar to you.

Terms used in mystical theology often carry very different definitions and nuances than the common-use definitions of the same words. As an example, in chapter eight of *Ascent of Mount Carmel*, St. John of the Cross discusses the difference between contemplation of the intellect and contemplation proper to mystical theology. There is a chasm between these two meanings that is often invisible to the inexperienced traveler, and confusion in this case is easy to come by. To mitigate these difficulties, you'll find an extensive glossary of terms in the appendix. It would be well worth the effort (if you have not already done so) to briefly review the glossary before digging into the next section.

DIAGNOSING YOUR CURRENT SPIRITUAL PROGRESS

Don't think of the following exercises as some kind of personality test, like those you might encounter in the workplace. Spiritual status and growth has eternal consequences, and your eternal destiny is at stake. Understanding who you are and where you are in light of your final destination is critical.

Therefore, don't take this work lightly. Just as with the root sin evaluation, it is best to pursue this exercise during or after a silent retreat, ideally before the Blessed Sacrament. It would be best to work through this self-evaluation with your spiritual director, which will prevent it from becoming a purely personal or isolated exercise subject to a measure of self-deception. In any case, here are five steps you can follow:

1. Spend time in prayer and ask the Holy Spirit to help you. This prayer may be helpful:

    Oh blessed Trinity, help me to know my deeds and myself without deception or duplicity. Save me, dear God, from falsehood and pretension, not only in the eyes of others but also in the depths of my soul. I am weak and faulty. Make me grow strong, holy, and honest with pure intention. I ask with humility to know the clarity of how I have sinned, how I have failed You and others. Most particularly I beg to know the roots and reasons and sources of my sins, to begin to see myself as I really am. To see the good You have accomplished in me, but also to acknowledge the deep flaws and weakness of character that lie under the surface of my behavior. What kind of person am

I? Oh God, tell me, tell me unsparingly. I wish to listen to You with all humility. Help me to be led by You to live a better and more holy life. Come, O Holy Spirit, fill my mind with light and my heart with honesty. Immaculate Mother of Christ and honest St. Joseph, please pray for me and help me. Amen.

2. If you have not already done so, review the glossary of terms so that you are able to clearly understand what the words mean.

3. Read the spiritual phases through completely one time. During this reading, underline those elements that seem to accurately reflect your current status.

4. Take a second pass but do so more carefully and prayerfully. If you think any item is possibly present in you, highlight it (if you have not already done so).

5. On the third and last pass, identify the phase that has the most markings—this will be a good start at identifying your relative location in the spiritual journey.

PRE-SPIRITUAL CHILDHOOD

The pre-infancy phase outlined here is not commonly identified in mystical or ascetical theology, because the soul at this stage has yet to enter the interior life in any meaningful way. It is likely that you will find yourself beyond these stages noted here; even so, it is helpful to review them and watch for signs of regression during your spiritual journey.

Hardened in Sin

- Mortal Sin: Stubborn persistence in sin either out of ignorance or because of a warped or severely underdeveloped conscience.
- Prayer: Deliberate refusal to have recourse to God for any manner of help or provision.
- Sacraments: Rarely attends Mass, if at all, and does not participate in Confession.

Surface Christianity

- Mortal Sin: Considered an insignificant nuisance and easily forgiven. The soul gives way to and commits mortal sin at every occasion or temptation. Confession, if practiced, is almost without remorse.

- Prayer: Mechanical and inattentive, last on the list of priorities, or easily abandoned by minor distractions or difficulty. These souls rarely enter into themselves in prayer, or do so superficially, and do not set aside or protect specific time for prayer on a daily basis.
- Sacraments: Sporadically attends Mass and Confession—often only at Easter and Christmas.

As we leave the outside of the castle and now begin to enter in, the following illustration reflects each key period of growth as we work toward union with God.

Unitive   VII: **Complete Sanctity**
          VI: **Heroic Perfection**

Illuminative   V: **Relative Perfection**
          IV: **Fervor**

Purgative   III: **Sustained Piety**
          II: **Intermittent Piety**
          I: **Mediocre Piety**

SPIRITUAL CHILDHOOD—THE PURGATIVE WAY

The entry into this first phase of the interior life begins with the most basic motivation to pursue God or a meaningful spiritual life. Often this motivation is rooted in fear and duty rather than love and devotion. Even though imperfect, with perseverance this can provide a healthy foundation for pilgrims seeking to deepen their faith. In this phase, the will is still very weak and prone to fall into sin. In this phase, we also regularly find energetic converts and reverts who have discovered or rediscovered their need for a deeper life of faith. In this phase, the properly disposed soul seeks to gain an awareness of its sins, deal with sorrow for past sins, and cultivate a strong desire to rid themselves of these offenses against God and neighbor. Accordingly, we begin to see here the initial efforts at prayer and piety. In this stage we'll explore three phases: *mediocre piety, intermittent piety*, and *sustained piety*, along with their manifestations.

Mediocre Piety

- Mortal Sin: Weak resistance. Rarely avoids near occasions of sin, but seriously regrets having sinned, and makes adequate confessions.
- Venial Sin: Considered insignificant and even at times embraced or desired. Hence the lukewarm state of the will. Does nothing whatever to prevent venial sin, or pays enough attention to avoid it, or uncover and uproot it when it is less conspicuous.
- Prayer: From time to time prays well, but still in an ad hoc fashion. Spiritual fervency is inconsistent and fleeting. Prayer is far from habitual but is valued, even if minimally so. Prayer is usually either intermittently attentive vocal prayer or a petition-based prayer focused on temporal needs and desires.
- Sacraments: Attends Mass regularly and pursues Confession more frequently.

Intermittent Piety

- Mortal Sin: Loyal resistance. Habitually avoids the near occasion of sin. Deeply regrets sin when recognized. Does penance to make reparation.
- Venial Sin: Sometimes deliberate. Puts up a weak fight. Sorrow is only superficial. Makes an examination of conscience, but without any method, preparation, or coherence.
- Prayer: Practices vocal prayer regularly. Not yet firmly resolved to remain faithful to structured meditation (time, place, topic, and material). Gives up as soon as dryness is felt, or as soon as there is business to attend to.
- Sacraments: Attends Mass weekly and pursues Confession at least quarterly.

Sustained Piety

- Mortal Sin: Never. At most very rare and only when taken suddenly by surprise and then, often it is to be doubted if the sin is mortal. It is followed by ardent feelings of guilt and a desire for penance.

- Venial Sin: Vigilant in avoiding and fighting it and rarely deliberate. Intense sorrow, but does little by way of reparation. Consistent particular examen, but aiming only at avoidance of venial sin.
- Imperfections: The soul either avoids uncovering them so as not to have to fight them, or else easily excuses them. Approves the thought of renouncing them, and would like to do so, but makes little effort in that direction.
- Prayer: Consistently faithful to specific time and approach to prayer, no matter what happens. This prayer includes vocal prayer and meditation that is often affective. Alternating consolations and dryness, the latter endured with considerable hardship.[2]
- Sacraments: Always attends weekly and daily Mass if able. Pursues Confession on a regular schedule.

SPIRITUAL ADOLESCENCE—THE ILLUMINATIVE WAY

The soul in spiritual adolescence is characterized by purposeful and consistent growth in prayer, virtue, love of neighbor, a deeper awakening of the mind and heart in the ways of God, and an increasingly clear understanding of God's will as it applies to a particular state of life. At this point, the struggle to overcome habitual sin, both mortal and venial, and the resulting increase in moral stability has, for the most part, been won. The soul has an ever-deepening desire for the heights of union with God and purity in thought, word, and deed. This phase is often preceded or occupied with significant suffering and purifications. However, the soul is also comforted with consolations and favors from God that sustain it through difficult times.

Fervor

- Venial Sin: Never deliberate. By surprise, sometimes, or with imperfect advertence. Keenly regretted and serious reparation made.
- Imperfections: Wants nothing to do with them. Watches over them, fights them with courage and diligence in order to be more

---

2. Note that though this level of maturity is still within the purgative stage, this is a significantly higher form of prayer than in the previous state and sometimes requires a great deal of time and energy to achieve, though God will ultimately decide how much progress is made regardless of the effort expended.

pleasing to God. Still, imperfections are sometimes accepted, though regretted at once. Frequent acts of renunciation. Particular examen aims at perfection in a specific virtue.

- Prayer: Vocal and mental prayer is constantly practiced and gladly prolonged. Prayer is often affective and the prayer of simplicity begins to emerge. Alternation between powerful consolations and fierce trials.

- Sacraments: Fervently participates in weekly and daily Mass if able. Pursues Confession at least on a monthly basis. Imperfections are offered in Confession for the purpose of obtaining the grace necessary to overcome them (i.e., devotional Confession).

Relative Perfection
- Imperfections: Guards against them energetically and with much care and love. They only happen with half-advertence.
- Prayer: Habitual life of prayer, even when occupied in external works. Thirst for self-renunciation, annihilation, detachment, and divine love. Hunger for the Eucharist and for heaven. Graces of infused prayer, of different degrees. Often passive purification.

SPIRITUAL ADULTHOOD—THE UNITIVE WAY

The principle feature of spiritual adulthood is a simple and constant awareness of God's presence and an obvious and habitual conformity to God's will. There is deep and abiding joy, a constant love for God and others, profound humility, freedom from the fear of suffering often accompanied by a strong desire to suffer for God, and apostolic fruitfulness. The suffering in this phase is more closely related to joining in the sufferings of Christ for the purposes of His redeeming grace rather than suffering for one's own sins. All of the virtuous developments previously acquired in the soul are assumed present here, thus the distinctions are simple.

Heroic Perfection
- Imperfections: Nothing but the first impulse.
- Prayer: Supernatural graces of contemplation sometimes accompanied by extraordinary phenomena. Pronounced passive purifications.

Contempt of self to the point of complete self-forgetfulness. Prefers suffering to joys.

Complete Sanctity
- Imperfections: Hardly apparent and rare.
- Prayer: Frequently experience the transforming union.

As we conclude this exploration of the three stages, it is worth noting that the vast majority of pilgrims will likely find themselves somewhere within the purgative way (spiritual childhood). If the drawbridge and door into the purgative way is prayer and a God-oriented self-knowledge (through reflection), the guarantee of passage is in perseverance and the grace of God (who promises to give Himself liberally to those who strive for holiness).

QUESTIONS FOR REFLECTION

As you study and reflect on the three stages, where do you see yourself?

If you have a spiritual director, explain why you feel it would be beneficial to review and work through identifying these stages together.

If you don't have a spiritual director, describe your plan for working on this process so as to avoid self-deception. Will you share this with a trusted spiritual companion? Someone who knows you very well? If you are resistant to this idea, why do you think this is so?

If you find yourself, like most pilgrims, in the spiritual childhood stage, how does this make you feel? Are you content to stay there, or do you feel convicted to move forward?

DEVELOPING A RULE OF LIFE

A "rule of life" (also referred to as a "program of life" or a "plan of life") is very beneficial to those journeying toward God. A rule of life, as applied to those of us who do not belong to a religious community, is more of a personalized creed or plan that acts as our "compass" and helps us to stay on the right path as determined through the spiritual evaluation exercises. Paragraph eighty-eight of *The Priest, Minister of Divine Mercy* says this about developing a plan for spiritual growth:

> The journey of spiritual direction can opportunely be embarked upon by a general revision of one's life. It is always useful to have a plan or some particular resolutions covering our relationship with God (liturgical and personal prayer), our fraternal relationships, the family, work, friendships, the specific virtues, our personal duties. Such plans can also reflect our aspirations, the difficulties we encounter, and the desire to give ourselves increasingly to God. It is very useful to indicate precisely the spiritual method which one intends to adopt for the journey towards prayer, holiness (virtue), the duties of state, mortification and for the minor daily hardships of life.

A good program or rule of life will include the following elements: period of time, root sin identification, corresponding virtue, virtue in Christ's life, prayer and the sacraments, and daily schedule. Here are some questions to assist you to begin to craft your own rule of life:

- What time period will this rule cover? Six months? One year?

- Knowing your root sin and how it manifests in your life, what corresponding virtue will you pursue to help fight your root sin that you identified in the previous chapter?
- How does that virtue manifest itself in the life and person of Christ? In what way is Christ's example specifically inspiring to you in your pursuit of holiness?
- How will you specifically attempt to live out that virtue?
- How do you plan to grow in faith through prayer and the sacraments?

A rule of life can be very detailed or very simple. From the simple end of the spectrum, you might write out your plan of life on one sheet of paper that reflects certain types of prayer and other commitments you will keep according to a specific schedule each day. An example of a brief focus point and a schedule might look like this:

Focus Point: This week I want to work on ensuring that I am gentle and respectful to my spouse and family—particularly when I get interrupted when I am trying to get work done. When the interruption comes, I will stop my work, turn to them, and engage with love and gentleness.

SCHEDULE:

7:00 a.m. to 7:10 a.m.	Meditation
7:10 a.m. to 7:20 a.m.	Scripture Reading and Reflection
7:20 a.m. to 7:30 a.m.	Decade of the Rosary
11:50 a.m. to 12:00 p.m.	Angelus
12:00 p.m. to 1:00 p.m.	Mass
4:30 p.m.	Start ramping down work for the day so I can leave on time
5:00 p.m.	Leave work to get home on time for dinner with family
6:00 p.m. to 7:00 p.m.	Dinner with Family/Rosary
8:30 p.m. to 8:45 p.m.	Examination of Conscience and Night Prayer

Bob chose an even simpler way to start. He wrote out how he would react when confronted with a frequent temptation he was struggling with. It looked like this:

Focus Point: Every time I have thoughts or temptation about _____, I will begin to pray the Hail Mary until they dissipate.

How will you live your rule of life on a daily basis? This might include specific times for morning prayer, other prayer, examination of conscience, and so on. This schedule could indicate which of the scheduled items are non-negotiable commitments, and which are optional in the sense that you wouldn't violate your rule of life if you were not able to accomplish them on any particular day. As you begin to develop your rule of life, keep in mind that a key ingredient is being as specific and focused as possible. Emphasis on everything is emphasis on nothing. If you can explain your rule of life to a stranger, you are probably clear enough. An acronym commonly used when creating goals is S.M.A.R.T: Are they Specific, Measurable, Actionable, Realistic, and Time-bound?

As you review your initial attempts to write up your rule of life, ask yourself the following questions:

- Are my spiritual goals precise, detailed, and explicit (specific)? In what way?
- Have I stated my spiritual goals in a way that I can easily determine if I have achieved them or not? Describe how.
- Is my rule of life clear enough that I can take daily steps toward achieving its various goals?
- Is my rule of life realistic and within reach for someone with my responsibilities as a mother/father, wife/husband, etc.?
- Is my rule of life tied to increments of time (days, weeks, months, or years) so I have the added benefit of working from a specific schedule?

One note of caution: This exercise is best done with the aid of a spiritual director. At the very minimum, you need the eyes of someone who has gone through this process and has a good understanding of the necessary components. As a last resort, you could work on this with a spouse or a trusted spiritual friend who can provide you with objective feedback.

Finally, regardless of the specific approach you take, at the end of each day you should do a brief examination of your rule of life with your night prayers. During this time you can review your focus points or any commitments you have made, you can thank God for any positive progress during the day or ask His forgiveness for the areas where you've failed, and you can jot down different ways you might make more progress tomorrow.

Rule of Life Worksheets

Root Sin	Opposite Virtue	Focus points
Common Manifestation	*How might it specifically manifest in my life?*	**S**pecific **M**easurable **A**ctionable **R**ealistic **T**ime Bound
Toward God	Toward God	PLAN OF ACTION
Toward Others	Toward Others	PLAN OF ACTION
Toward Myself	Toward Myself	PLAN OF ACTION

Notes:

Time/Period	Activity or Commitment

GLOSSARY OF TERMS

Unless otherwise noted, these terms are provided by *Modern Catholic Dictionary* by John A. Hardon, S.J. (Eternal Life Publications, 2000).

affective: See prayer, affective.

aridity: The state of a soul devoid of sensible consolation, which makes it very difficult to pray. It may be caused by something physical, such as illness, or voluntary self-indulgence, or an act of God, who is leading a person through trial to contemplation.

appetites, disordered: Inordinate and willful desires of created things or circumstances not rightly ordered to moral or spiritual good that impede union with God and darken, defile, weaken, and torment the soul (Author).

ascetical theology: The science of the saints based on a study of their lives. It is aimed to make people holy by explaining what sanctity is and how to attain it. It is the science of leading souls in the ways of Christian perfection through growth in charity and the practice of prayer leading to contemplation. It is that part of spiritual theology which concentrates on man's cooperation with grace and the need for human effort to grow in sanctity.

attachment: An emotional dependence, either of one person on another, or of a person on some real or illusory object. Attachments play an important role in spiritual development, since the first condition for progress in sanctity is some mastery over one's inordinate attachments.

confession, devotional: The practice of regular Confession even when one is not aware of mortal or even venial sins. This practice includes setting and keeping a specific schedule of self-examination and Confession. This may also include the confession of past mortal or venial sins, even if confessed previously in specific or in general. Devotional Confession can also make note of imperfections (see imperfections) though they are not sufficient matter for absolution. In such case, previously confessed sins, especially related to one's predominant fault, should be mentioned. Note: This practice is not recommended for those who suffer with scrupulosity (Author).

concupiscence: Insubordination of man's desires to the dictates of reason, and the propensity of human nature to sin as a result of original sin. More commonly, it refers to the spontaneous movement of the sensitive appetites toward whatever the imagination portrays as pleasant and away from whatever it portrays as painful. However, concupiscence also includes the unruly desires of the will, such as pride, ambition, and envy.

consolation: An interior movement aroused in the soul, by which it is inflamed with love of its Creator and Lord. It is likewise consolation when one sheds tears that move to the love of God, whether it is because of sorrow for sins, or because of the sufferings of Christ our Lord, or for any other reason that is immediately directed to the praise and service of God. Consolation can also be every increase of faith, hope, and love, and all interior joy that invites and attracts to what is heavenly and to the salvation of one's soul by filling it with peace and quiet in its Creator and Lord (adapted from St. Ignatius Spiritual Exercises, 316).

contemplation: See prayer, contemplation, infused.

detachment: In asceticism, the withholding of undue affection for creatures for the sake of the Creator. When mortal sin is involved, detachment is imperative for salvation. Detachment from creatures that are an obstacle to complete service of God is a normal condition for growth in holiness.

disposition: A quality or condition of the heart necessary for the performance of some action or of preparation for an encounter with the mysteries of God. Commonly applied to the conditions required for the valid reception or administration of the sacraments, as the state of grace is required for the Sacrament of the Eucharist, or sincere contrition to receive absolution in the Sacrament of Penance or a proper state of heart to enter into prayer and worship (Author).

disordered affections: See attachment.

Doctor of the Church: A title given since the Middle Ages to certain saints whose writing or preaching is outstanding for guiding the faithful in all periods of the Church's history.

dryness: See aridity.

examen: Reflection in God's presence on one's state of soul that has some reference to a specific adopted standard of conduct—i.e., rule of life or commitments, etc. (Author).

examen, particular: Regular prayerful examination of one's conscience by concentrating on some one particular moral failing to be overcome or virtue to be exercised. Its focus is on such external manifestations of the fault or virtue as can be remembered for periodic inventory. Particular examens are changed weekly, monthly, or otherwise, in order to ensure maximum attention. They are also commonly associated with some brief invocation for divine assistance, as occasions arise for avoiding a sin or acting on a virtue. And after some time another cycle may be started of the same defects that this person has to conquer or good habits he or she needs to develop.

examination of conscience: See examen.

formation: The act or process of developing someone in all realms of human experience but in particular those that help the human person come to better know and love God and serve others. Although human guides may assist or guide this process, we are "formed" by God, as illustrated through the imagery of the potter (God) and the clay (soul) (Author).

imperfections: Deficiencies of character that, although not as serious as mortal or venial sins, are nonetheless obstacles to attaining Christian perfection and union with God. The intentional omission of an obligatory good act is sinful (e.g., missing Mass on Sunday without sufficient reason). However, the failure to do a good act that is not obligatory (e.g., not going to daily Mass), whether through human frailty or the difficulty of judging its obligation, is considered a moral imperfection. While imperfections reflect deficiencies in our character and are obstacles to Christian perfection, they are not sins and therefore are insufficient matter for absolution. However, they may be confessed in order to settle one's conscience and to grow in the spiritual life. The scrupulous would constitute an exception, and should follow the guidance of their confessor or spiritual director in such matters (Author).

infused prayer: See prayer, contemplation, infused.

magisterium: The Church's teaching authority, vested in the bishops, as successors of the Apostles, under the Roman Pontiff, as successor of St. Peter. Also vested in the pope, as Vicar of Christ and visible head of the Catholic Church.

movement: An ecclesial organization with canonical recognition that provides defined paths to living out baptismal commitments, discipleship, and related sanctity through a specific spiritual lens called a "charism" that is expressed by distinctive practices of life and ways of prayer (Author).

mysticism: The supernatural state of soul in which God is known in a way that no human effort or exertion could ever succeed in producing. There is an immediate, personal experience of God that is truly extraordinary, not only in intensity and degree, but in kind. It is always the result of a special, totally unmerited grace of God. Christian mysticism differs essentially from the non-Christian mysticism of the Oriental world. It always recognizes that the reality to which it penetrates simply transcends the soul and the cosmos; there is no confusion between I and thou, but always a profound humility before the infinite Majesty of God. And in Christian mysticism all union between the soul and God is a moral union of love, in doing His will even at great sacrifice to self; there is no hint of losing one's being in God or absorption of one's personality into the divine.

orthodoxy: Right belief as compared with heterodoxy or heresy.

particular examen: See examen, particular.

piety: The religious sensibility of a person that reflects an attitude of reverence, respect, and devotion toward God and the things of God (Author).

penance: The virtue or disposition of heart by which one repents of one's own sins and is converted to God. Also the punishment by which one atones for sins committed, either by oneself or by others. And finally the Sacrament of Penance, where confessed sins committed after Baptism are absolved by a priest in the name of God.

prayer, contemplation, infused: An infused supernatural gift that originates completely outside of our will or ability, in God, by which a person becomes freely absorbed in God producing a real awareness, desire, and love for Him. This often gentle or delightful or sometimes non-sensible encounter can yield special insights into things of the spirit, resulting in a deeper and more tangible desire to love God and neighbor in thought, word, and deed. It is important to note that infused contemplation is a state that can be prepared for, but cannot in any way be produced by the will or desire of a person through methods or ascetical practices (Author).

prayer, meditation: Reflective prayer. The form of mental prayer in which the mind, in God's presence, thinks about God and divine things. While the affections may also be active, the stress in meditation is on the role of the intellect. Hence this is also called discursive mental prayer. The objects of meditation are mainly three: mysteries of faith; a person's better knowledge of what God wants him or her to do; and the divine will, to know how God wants to be served by the one who is meditating.

prayer, affective: Often the result of discursive meditation, affective prayer occurs when the heart and mind are engaged, with and beyond the intellect, with the object of the meditation (Author).

prayer, mental: The form of prayer in which the sentiments expressed are one's own and not those of another person, and the expression of these sentiments is mainly, if not entirely, interior and not externalized (e.g., not vocalized). Mental prayer is accomplished by internal acts of the mind and affections that are a loving and discursive (reflective) consideration of religious truths or some mystery of faith. In mental prayer the three powers of the soul are engaged: the memory, which offers the mind material for meditation; the intellect, which ponders or directly perceives the meaning of some religious truth and its implications for practice; and the will, which freely expresses its sentiments of faith, trust, and love, and (as needed) makes good resolutions based on what the memory and intellect have made known to the will (adapted from Hardon by the author).

prayer of simplicity: Meditation replaced by a purer, more intimate prayer consisting in a simple regard or loving thought on God, or on one of His attributes, or on some mystery of the Christian faith. The soul peacefully attends to the operations of the Spirit with sentiments of love without requiring the use of mental effort (adapted from Hardon).

prayer, vocal: Any form of prayer expressed audibly using pre-written formulas (e.g., Rosary, Liturgy of the Hours, etc.).

predominant fault: The defect in us that tends to prevail over the others, and thereby over our manner of feeling, judging, sympathizing, willing, and acting. This defect has in each of us an intimate relation to our individual temperament (see Lagrange, *Three Ages,* Part 2, chapter 22).

purification, active: This purification comes about as a result of the efforts of the soul (aided by the Holy Spirit) who seeks to purify itself from sins, vices, imperfections, and anything that would keep it from attaining holiness, union with God, and living a life that honors God and neighbor (Author).

purification, passive: This purification shares the same end as "active purification" whose means are solely of God and from God. This purification is the preparation for the exceptional graces of the supernatural life (Author).

program of life: See rule of life.

recollection: Concentration of the soul on the presence of God.

renunciation: To give up something to which a person has a claim. Some renunciations are necessary by divine law; others are permitted and encouraged according to divine counsel. Everyone must renounce sin and those creatures that are proximate occasions to sin. In this category belongs the renunciation of Satan at Baptism, either by the person being baptized or by the sponsor. Renunciations of counsel pertain to the exercise of such natural rights as material possessions, marriage, and legitimate autonomy or self-determination, sacrificed for love of God by those who vow themselves to poverty, chastity, and obedience.

reparation: The act or fact of making amends. It implies an attempt to restore things to their normal or sound conditions, as they were before something wrong was done. It applies mainly to recompense for the losses sustained or the harm caused by some morally bad action. With respect to God, it means making up with greater love for the failure in love through sin; it means restoring what was unjustly taken and compensating with generosity for the selfishness that caused the injury.

rule of life: A specific and usually documented plan for living in accord with one's state in life and baptismal commitments that includes principals, guidelines, and commitments that will guide each person to achieve sanctity, and in practical and concrete ways, love God and love their neighbor (Author). A principle or regular mode of action, prescribed by one in authority, for the well-being of those who are members of a society. In this sense the organized methods of living the evangelical counsels are called "rules," as the Rule of St. Augustine or the Rule of St. Benedict. A rule may also be a customary standard that is not necessarily prescribed by authority, but voluntarily undertaken in order to regulate one's conduct for more effective moral living or more effective service of others.

root sin: See predominant fault.

scrupulosity: The habit of imagining sin where none exists, or grave sin where the matter is venial. To overcome scrupulosity, a person needs to be properly instructed in order to form a right conscience, and in extreme cases the only remedy is absolute obedience (for a time) to a prudent confessor.

self-knowledge: Personal awareness of both the dignity of the human soul and its exalted destiny, as well as knowledge of the wounds and darkness that original and personal sin has inflicted on it. This awareness is not one that is isolated to the natural order but that frames self-understanding in the context of God's presence and God's law (Author).

self-denial: The act or practice of giving up some legitimate satisfaction for the sake of some higher motive.

self-renunciation: See renunciation.

self-annihilation: Heroic renunciation and self-giving. See renunciation.

sin, mortal: An actual sin that destroys sanctifying grace and causes the supernatural death of the soul. Mortal sin is a turning away from God because of a seriously inordinate adherence to creatures that causes grave injury to a person's rational nature and to the social order, and deprives the sinner of a right to heaven. The terms mortal, deadly, grave, and serious applied to sin are synonyms, each with a slightly different implication. Mortal and deadly focus on the effects in the sinner, namely deprivation of the state of friendship with God; grave and serious refer to the importance of the matter in which a person offends God. But the Church never distinguishes among these terms as though they represented different kinds of sins. There is only one recognized correlative to mortal sin, and that is venial sin, which offends against God but does not cause the loss of one's state of grace.

sin, near occasion of: Any person, place, or thing that of its nature or because of human frailty can lead one to do wrong, thereby committing sin. If the danger is certain and probable, the occasion is proximate; if the danger is slight, the occasion becomes remote. It is voluntary if it can easily be avoided. There is no obligation to avoid a remote occasion unless there is probable danger of its becoming proximate. There is a positive obligation to avoid a voluntary proximate occasion of sin even though the occasion of evildoing is due only to human weakness.

sin, root sin: See predominant fault.

sin, venial: An offense against God which does not deprive the sinner of sanctifying grace. It is called venial (from *venia pardon*) because the soul still has the vital principle that allows a cure from within, similar to the healing of a sick or diseased body whose source of animation (the soul) is still present to restore the ailing bodily function to health. Deliberate venial sin is a disease that slackens the spiritual powers, lowers one's resistance to evil, and causes one to deviate from the path that leads to heavenly glory. Variously called "daily sins" or "light sins" or "lesser sins," they are committed under a variety of conditions: when a person transgresses with full or partial knowledge and consent to a divine law that does not oblige seriously; when one violates a law that obliges gravely but either one's knowledge or consent is not complete; or when one disobeys what is an objectively grave precept, but due to invincible ignorance a person thinks the obligation is not serious. The essence of venial sin consists in a certain disorder but does not imply complete aversion from humanity's final destiny. It is an illness of the soul rather than its supernatural death. When people commit a venial sin, they do not decisively set themselves on turning away from God, but from over-fondness for some created good fall short of God. They are like persons who loiter without leaving the way.

spiritual exercises: Any set program of religious duties, notably the prayers, meditations, and spiritual reading required of persons following a distinctive rule of life. Also the period of silence and prayerful reflection practiced annually (or more often) in a retreat. Particularly the spiritual exercises by St. Ignatius Loyola, drawn up as a method of arriving at the amendment of one's life and resolving on a determined way of holiness. The exercises of St. Ignatius were first composed by him in a cave at Manresa, in Spain, after his conversion. They have been recommended by successive popes as a most effective program of spiritual renewal for priests, religious, and the laity. Their underlying principle is their opening statement that "Man was created to praise, reverence and serve our Creator and Lord, and by this means to save his soul." Given this basic purpose of human existence, the believer is told how to reach his or her destiny by overcoming sinful tendencies and imitating Christ in carrying the Cross on earth, in order to be glorified with Christ in the life to come.

spiritual marriage: See transforming union.

spiritual warfare: A form of prayer and personal vigilance, with humble reliance on the grace and power of God, that sets itself specifically and actively against particular forces of evil as they manifest themselves in the flesh and the world (Author).

transforming union: The highest degree of perfection attained in this life, marked by a total transformation of the soul into the Beloved, wherein God and the soul give themselves to each other in the ultimate consummation of divine love (Author; adapted from *Spiritual Theology*, Jordan Aumann [New York: Continuum, 2006], 350–351).

third order: Associations of the faithful established by religious orders. Dating from the thirteenth century, they may be either secular or regular. If secular, they are laypersons, commonly called tertiaries. If regular, they are religious, bound by public vows and living in community. Originally, third orders were Franciscan or Dominican, but the Holy See has since approved many others, both secular and regular—e.g., the Augustinians, Carmelites, Servites, and Trinitarians.

Are you looking to deepen your faith and relationship with God?

AVILA INSTITUTE

FOR SPIRITUAL FORMATION

The mission of the Avila Institute is to provide spiritual education and formation to Catholics around the world who are seeking to deepen their understanding and appropriation of the magisterium-faithful, mystical and ascetical patrimony of the Catholic Church.

With online instructors from around the country, the Avila Institute provides online instruction that cannot be found anywhere else!

www.Avila-Institute.com

Questions? Contact our Admissions Department:

admissions@myavila.com

SPIRITUAL DIRECTION
⇒ SERIES ⇐

SOPHIA INSTITUTE PRESS

If this book has caused a stir in your heart to continue to pursue your relationship with God, we invite you to explore two extraordinary resources, SpiritualDirection.com and the Avila Institute for Spiritual Formation.

The readers of SpiritualDirection.com reside in almost every country of the world where hearts yearn for God. It is the world's most popular English site dedicated to authentic Catholic spirituality.

The Students of the Avila Institute for Spiritual Formation sit at the feet of the rich and deep well of the wisdom of the saints.

You can find more about the Avila Institute at
WWW.AVILA-INSTITUTE.COM.

Sophia Institute

Sophia Institute is a nonprofit institution that seeks to nurture the spiritual, moral, and cultural life of souls and to spread the Gospel of Christ in conformity with the authentic teachings of the Roman Catholic Church.

Sophia Institute Press fulfills this mission by offering translations, reprints, and new publications that afford readers a rich source of the enduring wisdom of mankind.

Sophia Institute also operates the popular online resource CatholicExchange.com. *Catholic Exchange* provides world news from a Catholic perspective as well as daily devotionals and articles that will help readers to grow in holiness and live a life consistent with the teachings of the Church.

In 2013, Sophia Institute launched Sophia Institute for Teachers to renew and rebuild Catholic culture through service to Catholic education. With the goal of nurturing the spiritual, moral, and cultural life of souls, and an abiding respect for the role and work of teachers, we strive to provide materials and programs that are at once enlightening to the mind and ennobling to the heart; faithful and complete, as well as useful and practical.

Sophia Institute gratefully recognizes the Solidarity Association for preserving and encouraging the growth of our apostolate over the course of many years. Without their generous and timely support, this book would not be in your hands.

www.SophiaInstitute.com
www.CatholicExchange.com
www.SophiaInstituteforTeachers.org

Sophia Institute Press® is a registered trademark of Sophia Institute.
Sophia Institute is a tax-exempt institution as defined by the
Internal Revenue Code, Section 501(c)(3). Tax I.D. 22-2548708.